To:

SUNDAY PUNDAY

ESPRESSO YOURSELF

Artwork by Winsor Kinkade

HARVEST HOUSE PUBLISHERS
EUGENE, OREGON

SUNDAY PUNDAY

Copyright © 2016 Winsor Kinkade
Published by Harvest House Publishers
Eugene, Oregon 97402
www.harvesthousepublishers.com

978-0-7369-6788-4

Design by Dugan Design Group

*The H.J. Heinz Company, LP and Elmer's Products, Inc.
are not associated with the book.*

Printed in China

16 17 18 19 20 21 22 23 24 / RDS / 10 9 8 7 6 5 4 3 2 1

A Word from the Artist

There is an old adage that states, "Good artwork provokes emotion." My drawings in *Sunday Punday* were created with that phrase in mind, hoping to provoke in my viewers feelings of peace, inspiration, and laughter.

Each one of us is so different. We possess various talents, activities we enjoy, and passions that tug at our heart. However, the appreciation of beauty and finding humor within our world is something we can all share.

With this book, I hope to remind readers of the simple joys life holds. It's meant to inspire readers to love (and be loved) and offer a few moments in which we don't have to take ourselves so seriously.

Winsor

YOU'RE A GEM

wise Chinese proverb says that "the gem cannot be polished without friction, nor man perfected without trials." A gem doesn't just appear—*poof!*—flawlessly set in a necklace or impeccably cradled in a band of gold. The beauty of the gem is realized in the process—the time it takes to cut its perfect shape, to polish its brilliance, to select an ideal setting that brings its most luminous features to the forefront. It seems that the more rigorous the finishing process, the more radiant the gem. It takes faith and patience and vision to transform a gem. The undertaking may be intense, but the final product is priceless.

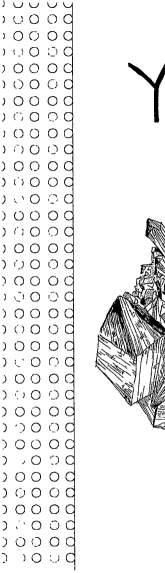

YOU'RE A

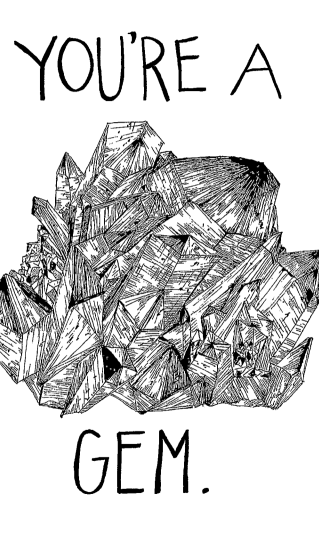

GEM.

LOVE WINS

(T)he painter Vincent van Gogh once said, "There is
nothing more truly artistic than to love people." Allow
that to sink in for a moment. *Love as art.* As personal
expression. As a brushstroke of creativity. Love your
friends. Love your family. Love the people you encounter
only once. Love your pets. Love yourself. Imagine.
Invent. Dream. Let the art of loving others permeate your
life. Know that there's no act of love too small
to be appreciated, nothing too insignificant to lift
someone's mood and put a smile in their heart. Every
day is an opportunity to express your heart.

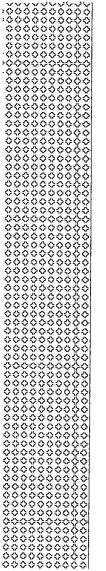

YOU ARE

BERRY SWEET.

YOU ARE BERRY SWEET

The perceptive pioneer writer Laura Ingalls Wilder once said, "It is the sweet, simple things of life which are the real ones after all." The sweetness of the berry is cultivated with the simple trio of light, water, and warmth. The sweetness of a soul, of a friendship, of a moment, is not difficult to discover if you look for the little things. A discovery in the details. A pause in the perseverance. A quietness in the clamor. A handful of berries can taste sweeter than the most decadent dessert, depending on how you're looking at it. When you embrace the simple, you taste the sweet.

YOU ARE MY ROCK

(W) hen you're out hiking in the mountains, radiant hues and impressive images capture your eye—the shimmer of a waterfall, the daintiness of wildflowers, a verdant canopy of foliage. Often, you don't notice the base of the mountain until maybe a loose stone makes you stumble. But everything relies upon the rock. Without it, there's no foundation. No place for those trees and flowers to take root. No formation for that ribbon of water to cascade down. No solid ground for the forest animals to scamper across and discover their burrows in. All things depend upon the solidity of the rock.

YOU'RE MY TYPE

(W)hether you're searching for a best friend or a soulmate, it's easy to write someone off as "not my type." But anyone can be your type...if you just find the correct keys. You can find threads of connection with anyone on this wide, wonderful planet. Begin by asking questions. Listening to the responses. Opening up a little—and then a little more. Sharing a dream—and sharing a little deeper. Laughing at something that strikes you as funny—and looking for reflected laughter. Reaching out—and discovering that surprising yet satisfying connection of being exactly the right type.

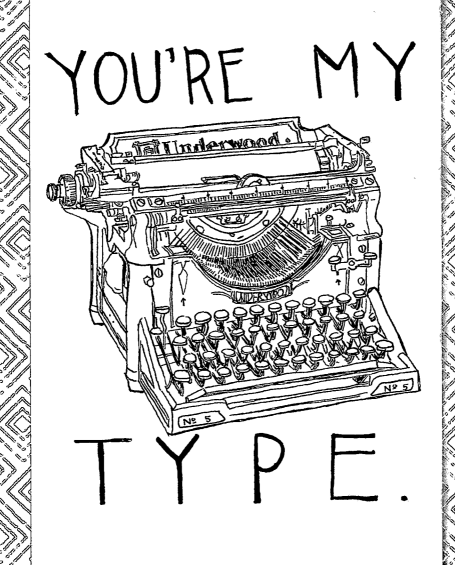

UNBEELIEVABLE

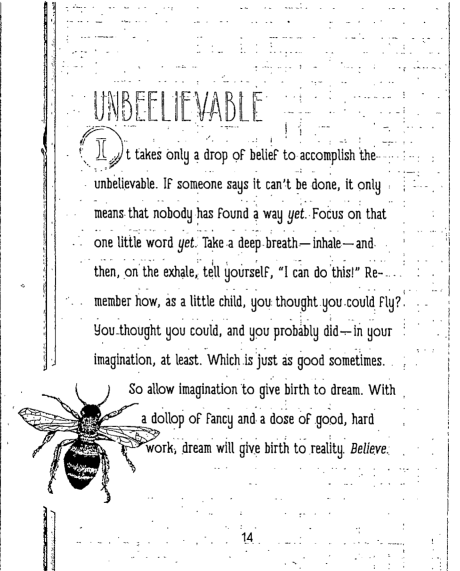

It takes only a drop of belief to accomplish the unbelievable. If someone says it can't be done, it only means that nobody has found a way *yet*. Focus on that one little word *yet*. Take a deep breath—inhale—and then, on the exhale, tell yourself, "I can do this!" Remember how, as a little child, you thought you could fly? You thought you could, and you probably did—in your imagination, at least. Which is just as good sometimes.

So allow imagination to give birth to dream. With a dollop of fancy and a dose of good, hard work, dream will give birth to reality. *Believe.*

UNBEELIEVABLE

DON'T BE CRABBY

Even if you're the happiest person on earth, you can still slip into a bad mood. While you don't need to be grinning 24/7, it's good to know what to do to get rid of the grumpies. Walk yourself out of the doldrums. Work out. Call a friend. Read a devotional or a book of inspiring quotes. Do some art. Smile—it will trigger happy chemicals in your brain. (Seriously!) Turn on some music, and then turn it up. Dip into that stash of treats you keep on hand for difficult days—your favorite bubble bath, a decadent chocolate sprinkled with sea salt, chamomile tea in your monogrammed mug. Feel the happiness beginning to seep into your spirit, and soak in the sunshine of renewal.

HAPPY AS A CLAM

(H)appy people have one thing in common: They know it's not all about them. Ralph Waldo Emerson once said, "Happiness is a perfume you cannot pour on others without getting a few drops on yourself." Instead of searching for happiness, start creating it yourself. That begins with refusing to compare yourself to others. Don't even go there. Instead, practice gratitude. Write down everything you're thankful for—big things and small. Even if it's just a list of little things, they add up to something grand. Practice asking the words, "How can I help you?" Step out of your shell and share a smile. Allow your happiness to spill out of your heart and into the hearts of others.

YOU TICKLE MY FANCY

Your best friends live your story with you. They're the ones who believe in you. Always. Even when you don't believe in yourself. When you ask for a best friend's honest opinion, you'll get it. Even if it's not the feedback you were hoping for. But that's okay because it's honest. Together, your laughter is louder. Your smiles are brighter. You have fun, even when you're not doing much of anything at all. You never run out of things to discuss, to ponder, to wonder. Maybe even better, you never run out of jokes. You tickle each other's fancy. And that's just the way it should be.

YOU TICKLE

MY FANCY.

I WHEELY LIKE YOU

Y ou're not perfect—far from it. But those who love you think you are. Or, rather, they accept you despite your lack of perfection. Because we all know that nobody is perfect. All of us have our quirks and eccentricities and imperfections. And it's actually those traits that can endear us to others. Like Mr. Knightley said to Emma in a film adaptation of Jane Austen's book, "Perhaps it is our imperfections that make us so perfect for each other." When we really like each other, we give each other grace. We forgive. We brush off a poorly chosen comment or an accidental slight. We choose to see the good in each other.

22

YOU MAKE LIFE BEARABLE

When life looks like it's not getting any better, that's when you need to reach out in faith to those who lift you up. Surround yourself with the people who tell you, "You can do it!" Hold fast to the friends who remind you, "I've got you. I'm not going to let you go." When you're with those who make the unbearable manageable if not easy, you know you're going to make it through the storm. As Martin Luther King Jr. said, "Faith is taking the first step, even when you don't see the whole staircase." Let your faith be bigger than your fear.

SNOW PLACE
LIKE HOME.

SNOW PLACE LIKE HOME

(T) here is nothing like staying at home for real comfort," Jane Austen wrote. At the close of a crazy day, home awaits us—a cat curled up on the sofa, a fireplace ready to be lit, baskets of books and mugs of warm drinks. Even when we're not at home, we're still drawn there. Oliver Wendell Holmes was right when he said, "Where we love is home—home that our feet may leave, but not our hearts." Home is a place, but it's also a feeling, a memory triggered by certain sights and sounds and smells. Home is where you feel the most like *you* and you're loved, accepted, and welcomed. *Home.*

I LOVE EWE

(T) ake a deep breath. Let go. Dive in. *Love*. Take risks.
Laugh out loud. Open your eyes. Notice the vivid hues sur-
rounding you and attune yourself to the most intricate details.
Appreciate. Be grateful. Drink it in. "You know you're in love
when you can't fall asleep because reality is finally better
than your dreams," said the one-of-a-kind Dr. Seuss. Maybe
you're consumed with love for another individual. Or a wild,
undiscovered place. Or a brand-new way of being.
You skip where you once walked. You climb where
you once stood still. You dance in the rain. Dive
off the rock. Reach for the star—and catch it. *Love*.

I LOVE EWE.

LET'S KETCHUP

(I) t is one of the blessings of old friends that you can afford to be stupid with them," said Ralph Waldo Emerson. There's an ease you settle into when getting together with an old friend—like slipping on your most comfortable pajamas or rereading your favorite book. Cozy. Snug. Agreeable. When you're finally back together, you're inseparable—munching your favorite foods, revisiting your favorite spots, finishing each other's sentences. And when you're separated for a week, a year, or longer? While your lives and your dreams and your styles may have changed quite a lot, your bond remains steadfast and solid as ever.

YOU OTTER BE KIDDING ME

It may sound like an otterly adorable myth, but it's true—otters hold hands when they sleep. Afloat on their backs, if one accidentally lets go, the other will grab back on so as not to let each other drift apart. If you've seen otters when they're awake, this may surprise you a bit. These carefree critters are known for their playfulness, their lightness, their flitting about. But when they're finally settled in and calmed down, otters instinctively know it's time to hang on for safety. And they immediately seek out their closest friends—other lighthearted souls. Together, they form a solid raft of safety.

ESPRESSO YOURSELF

(T) he best you is the expressed you—the you who isn't afraid to show off your own unique blend of personality and passions and panache. As the illustrious Dr. Seuss said, "Be who you are and say what you feel because those who mind don't matter and those who matter don't mind." So go ahead and write poetry. Dance. Sing. Twirl. Draw. Color. Paint. Hike. Run. Wander. Stretch. Dream. Grow. Accept yourself. Tell yourself, *You have value. You are blessed. You are creative.* And then go share that creativity with the world—or just with yourself. Express yourself however you like.

ESPRESSO YOURSELF.

I DIG YOU

In her beloved novel *Anne of Green Gables*, L.M. Montgomery painted the ultimate picture of a BFF: "True friends are always together in spirit." Anne's term for these special friends—kindred spirits—defined those individuals with whom we share a rare and special connection. And, as Anne discovered, maybe those who truly "get" each other aren't so rare after all: "Kindred spirits are not so scarce as I used to think. It's splendid to find out there are so many of them in the world." Be open to new friendships. Look for them in unexpected places. You might just discover a kindred spirit.

I'M QUITE FAWNED OF YOU

(I) t seems they had always been, and would always be, friends. Time could change much, but not that." There's perhaps no more beloved friendship in the pages of a book than the friendship between Winnie the Pooh and Piglet. A.A. Milne understood the meaning of *fondness*—of that unbreakable bond of togetherness and devoted companionship and unequaled contentment with each other. It's one thing to like someone; it's quite another to be fond of them. You can't impress someone enough to make them fond of you. Fondness must come from within—it wells up and bubbles over, like a belly laugh that can't be held back. Where there is fondness, there is joy.

I'm quite FAWNED of you.

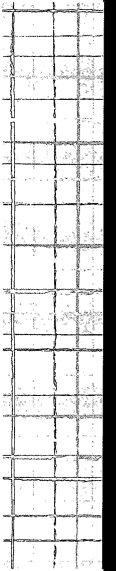

STICK TOGETHER

True friends are like the best kind of glue—they stick with you through the happy times, the stressful times, the confusing times, the silly times. As Alexandre Dumas wrote in *The Three Musketeers*, "All for one and one for all." When the world seems overwhelming or you aren't sure of the next step to take, know that those who care about you have you covered with their love and their prayers and their best thoughts. And when it's their turn to feel anxiety or pressure or joy, you can be the glue they need. When you stick together, you can get through anything.

WE'D MAKE A GREAT PEAR

Have you ever had that moment when you made a sure and sudden connection with another individual and just knew you'd be inseparable? "Friendship is born at that moment when one person says to another, 'What! You too? I thought I was the only one,'" wrote C.S. Lewis. Maybe you bonded over a favorite book. Perhaps you shared the same view on an important issue. Or you both like to rejuvenate in the same natural space. But there's even more than having something in common. It's that undefinable something inside each of you that just knows the other. That realizes the two of you are truly a matched pair.

DON'T BE SHELLFISH

The best gift you can give is the gift of yourself—your time, your talents, your presence. Even if you don't consider yourself wealthy in any way, you can still give. As Anne Frank wrote, "No one has ever become poor by giving." Your friendship is valuable. Your smile is of great worth. Your laughter, shared with another, can change someone's day—or maybe their life. Generosity is contagious. Once given away, it keeps growing and increasing in value. "The meaning of life is to find your gift," said the artist Pablo Picasso. "The purpose of life is to give it away."

I'M STUMPED.

I'M STUMPED

(C) onfused. Stuck. Undecided. In a rut. Trying to figure out the next step. Sometimes you want someone else to make up your mind for you. But making decisions is an inevitable part of life. And, as the wise Mark Twain observed, "Good decisions come from experience. Experience comes from making bad decisions." So you've gotta decide something, anything. But before you make that decision, ask yourself a few things. *Am I making this decision for myself or for someone else? Am I willing to have the courage to stick to my decision? Am I going to be at peace with this decision?* Then take a deep breath and follow your heart.

WE'VE GOT THYME

Hurry, *hurry, hurry,* shouts the world as text messages ping and timers ding and cell phones sing, sing, sing. It may sound like crazy advice, but it's okay to take your time. You don't have to respond right away. Allow yourself to think about things. Reflect for a while before choosing a course of action. Take a break to write a poem or listen to a song or go for a walk. Send a hand-written note instead of an email. Think about your words before you speak them—and sometimes choose not to say anything at all. Trace the movement of the clouds with your eyes. Watch a honeybee sip nectar from a flower. Life takes time.

OWL ALWAYS
BE THERE
FOR YOU.

OWL ALWAYS BE THERE FOR YOU

"Never be so busy as not to think of others," said Mother Teresa. It's easy to constantly be thinking of other people yet never quite taking that step of truly being there for them. We have so many demands on our time— projects and deadlines and commitments. All good things. But all our things. So go one step further with your caring and compassion and do something that makes a difference. Bake a batch of cookies for your stressed-out friend. Write a note of gratitude to your mom and dad. Buy a stranger a cup of coffee. Hold a hand. Listen. Simply be there.

SNAILED IT.

SNAILED IT

eonard da Vinci noted, "It had long since come to my attention that people of accomplishment rarely sat back and let things happen to them. They went out and happened to things." Every accomplishment, every exploit, every victory, starts with the decision to try—and then keep trying. So believe you can do it—and you will. For, according to the visionary Walt Disney, "If you dream it you can do it." If you need to, write down the steps to making your goal a reality. But then get busy putting in the effort, checking the items off your list, making forward progress. And then celebrate your success!

AHEAD YOU

Nobody was designed to go it alone. We need companions throughout life's journey. Peas in a pod. Partners in crime. Kindred spirits. Joined at the hip. Whatever you want to call it, the sentiment is the same. We're connected. Like the Roman poet and philosopher Lucretius so poignantly put it, "We are each of us angels with only one wing, and we can only fly by embracing one another." While our culture might champion individuality and every-man-for-himself, that's not the way things work best. We need each other to bounce ideas off of, to hold each other accountable, to pick us up when we fall. We're better together.

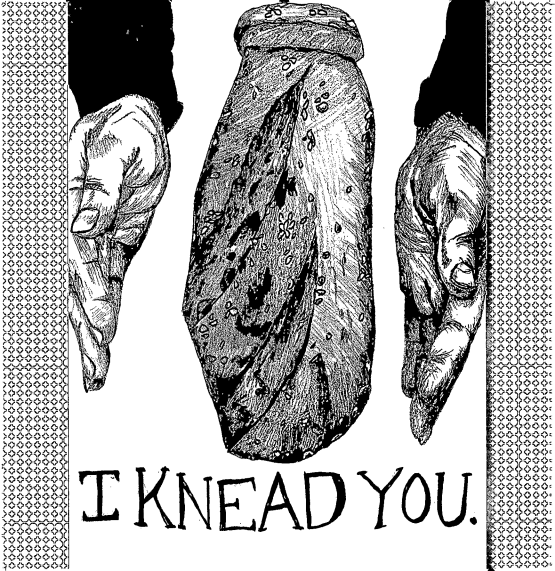

GOPHER IT

"Twenty years from now you will be more disappointed by the things that you didn't do than by the ones you did do, so throw off the bowlines, sail away from safe harbor, catch the trade winds in your sails. Explore. Dream. Discover," wrote Mark Twain. If that's not permission to go for it, I don't know what is. See the big picture. Cast your net wide. Don't be afraid to step out into the world. Refuse to let your fears and anxieties speak louder than your aspirations and ambitions. Where others see roadblocks, discover an interesting detour. Defy the limits. Launch yourself.

PIECE OF CAKE

Cake. It's the taste of celebration. The flavor of fun. Julia Child once said that "a party without cake is just a meeting." So say yes to that piece of cake. In fact, every now and then, have dessert first. And once in a while, eat cake for breakfast. Life is short, so say certainly to spontaneity. Accept that second helping. As a favorite saying goes, "There's always time for tea and there's always room for cake." And "saving room for cake" doesn't just mean dressing up your dinner. It's taking five minutes to paint your nails. Riding your bike instead of driving. Seeing where that trail leads. Saying yes to the moment, yes to living life.

PIECE OF

CAKE.

TAKE THE HIGH ROAD

When you're hurt, it's a natural reaction to lash out. To want to hurt back. To try to protect yourself. And while it's important to keep yourself safe, it's just as vital to keep yourself whole. You do this by taking the high road. React in a different way. In an unconventional manner. Forgive. Show kindness. Speak truth. Accept some of the blame. Ignore the gossip. Refuse to give a reaction. Maintain your integrity. Keep your focus. Choose to have a positive outlook. When you take the high road, you remove yourself from the distractions and make it easier to move on.

WINE NOT?

You see things; and you say, 'Why?' But I dream things that never were; and I say, 'Why not?'" penned the Irish playwright George Bernard Shaw. So why not? And why not right away? Why not do something you love, attempt something you've always wanted to try? Sign up for that class. Learn to play that instrument. Start training for that race. Plan that gathering of friends. Join that volunteer organization. There doesn't have to be any practical purpose or definite goal. If you never take the chance, you'll never know what your life might be missing. So why not?